THE LOON

BY
JUDITH PINKERTON JOSEPHSON

EDITED BY
JUDY LOCKWOOD

PUBLISHED BY
CRESTWOOD HOUSE
Mankato, MN, U.S.A.

C|P

LIBRARY OF CONGRESS CATALOGING IN PUBLICATION DATA

Josephson, Judith Pinkerton.
  The loon

  (Wildlife, habits & habitat)
  Includes index.
  SUMMARY: Describes the physical characteristics, behavior, lifestyle and natural environment of
the beautiful, graceful loon, one of the oldest birds on earth.
  1. Loon—Juvenile literature. [1. Loons] I. Lockwood, Judy, II. Title. III. Series.
QL696.G33J67   1988   598.4′42—dc19   88-9599
ISBN 0-89686-390-5

International Standard Book Number:	Library of Congress Catalog Card Number:
0-89686-390-5	88-9599

PHOTO CREDITS:

Cover: DRK Photo: Wayne Lankinen
Tom Stack & Associates: (Robert C. Simpson) 9; (Alan Nelson) 10, 14;
  (Dominique Braud) 13, 24
DRK Photo: (Wayne Lynch) 4; (Wayne Lankinen) 6, 19, 22, 30, 33,
  42-43; (Stephen J. Krasemann) 16, 21, 26-27, 29, 37, 39, 41;
  (John R. Hicks) 34-35

Produced by Carnival Enterprises.

CRESTWOOD·HOUSE

Box 3427, Mankato, MN, U.S.A. 56002

TABLE OF CONTENTS

INTRODUCTION:

It is early morning in the north woods. A large graceful bird, riding low in the water, glides across the calm lake. Suddenly an eerie, ringing call, like someone wildly laughing, fills the summer air. The notes echo through the pine forest. It is the unforgettable voice of the loon.

There's something magical about loons. For hundreds of years, people have been drawn by their beauty and unusual cackling calls. Loons make people think of the quiet wonder of the wilderness and the peacefulness of woods, lakes, and streams.

Native Americans honored the loon by creating ceremonial masks, totem poles, and fishing floats (to hold up their nets) in the shape of loons. Artists draw loons on stationery, clothing, and dishes.

The loon is one of the oldest birds on earth. Birds similar to the loon have been on the earth about 90 million years. Today, loons are much the same as when they first appeared.

The loon is a powerful diver, swimmer, and flier. With their splashy running take offs, these water birds seem to dance on top of the water. Loons breed and raise their young in the north, then migrate south to warmer coastal waters for the winter.

The loon is one the oldest birds on earth.

CHAPTER ONE

The loon is a large, duck-like water bird found in northern North America and Europe. There are four kinds of loons in the loon family (*Gaviidae*): the common loon, the arctic loon, the red-throated loon, and the yellow-billed loon.

The bones of a loon are heavier than other land birds.

Clumsy and graceful

Loons have long sturdy beaks, smooth heads, and bright red eyes. From far away, loons look black. But up close, their bodies are splashed with black and white in patterns of checks and stripes.

The word "loon" means "clumsy" or "awkward." On land, loons *are* clumsy. A loon's legs are set far back on its body and that makes walking difficult. The loon almost drags itself from the water to its nest.

In the water, loons are graceful. Their bodies and webbed toes are perfect for swimming, fishing, and diving. Their leg muscles blend smoothly into their bodies. They can swim fast, dive deeply, and turn quickly underwater.

Loons have enormous feet for their size. Each foot is five inches (13 centimeters) long and three inches (7.6 cm) wide. If a person's feet were that big for his size, he would have to wear clown shoes! The loon's feet push through the water like two big paddles.

As water birds, loons have heavier bones than land birds. That helps the bird dive and swim, but hinders its lifting into the air. The bones of land birds have tiny air sacs inside, which are little pockets of air that help the birds breathe and make them lighter in flight. The loon's air sacs are simpler and smaller.

Loons weigh about 7 to 14 pounds (1.8 to 6.3

kilograms), depending on the kind of loon. In spite of their weight, loons can fly long distances.

The body feathers of the loon are close together and thick. Feathers on the head and neck are soft and velvety, making a loon look like it's wearing a smooth cap over its head.

Bird feathers wear out and must be replaced each year with new ones. This process is called molting. Molting occurs in the fall, when loons shed their colorful breeding feathers. The shedding begins on the bird's chin and continues to its neck, forehead, and back. Dull brown winter feathers quickly grow in. After loons fly south, they molt their flight feathers. In March or April, loons shed again, changing back into their bright breeding feathers.

Birds of the north

There is a large loon population in Minnesota (10,000 loons), where it is the state bird. There are fewer loons in Maine, Wisconsin, and other northern states. Many loons live farther north in Alaska (270,000) and Canada (500,000).

Loons live on marshes, ponds, slow-moving rivers, and lakes. Almost any kind of lake will do for a home, but the water must be clear for diving and fishing.

Each loon needs about 30 acres (12 hectares) of

Marshes, ponds, and slow-moving waters are a loon's favorite habitats.

space. By comparison, robins need only a half-acre (0.2 hectares) to raise a family. Eagles need 2,000 acres (810 hectares). If a lake is large, several pairs of loons or a pair and a few single loons can live comfortably together. On a small lake, one pair of loons might claim the whole lake.

The call of the loon

The call of the loon sounds mysterious, romantic, scary, or sad. To some people, the loon's call might be

Tall weeds and grass protect the loons' nest.

an eerie howl, wild laughter, low cooing, or a long throaty yell. To others, the call is music.

On summer nights loons call to each other and fill the air with a chorus of calls which can be heard five miles (8 kilometers) away.

The loon calls by vibrating the syrinx (pronounced SIR-ingks), a simple vocal organ in the lower part of its windpipe. Loons talk to each other with their calls. The tremolo call sounds like someone who has heard a very good joke and can't stop laughing. The tremolo call signals that the loon has spotted its mate or that it is ready to take off. Loons also use the tremolo to communicate while they fly.

Another call, a sad low wail, is often heard at night. The loon could be telling its mate to trade places warming the eggs in the nest. This wail could also be a way of joining other loons in song.

Male loons give a wild yodel to attract the attention of a female or to warn another male to go away. The loon bends its head down low in the water with its neck and head flat to the water and its bill tipped up slightly.

The hoot is a quiet call, used between members of a loon family. Adults may hoot to call their chicks in for feeding.

Loon behavior

Loons are curious birds. They are nosy about what's going on in their territory. They'll swim over to investigate a sound, a rustling water plant, an animal, or anything else that looks suspicious. Many years ago, when loons were shot for sport, hunters took advantage of this curiosity to trick loons into coming close to shore.

Loons spend nearly two hours each day preening their feathers. Using their long beaks, the loons poke among their feathers, picking out insects. While preening, loons spread oil from a gland at the base of their tails over their feathers. The oil keeps their feathers glossy and waterproof. Sometimes loons preen each others' feathers, especially if they're trading egg-sitting duties.

When loons aren't preening, they're resting or fishing. Loons can dive underwater with very little effort. When a swimming loon is frightened, it glides along with only its head and bill showing above the water.

CHAPTER TWO:

Of the 8,000 different kinds of birds on earth, four are in the loon family. All four kinds of loons eat, raise their young, and live their lives in much the same way. They differ only in size, location, and color of breeding feathers.

The common loon

The best-known loon is the common loon. It has many nicknames: great northern diver, ring-necked loon, black-billed loon, ember goose, and walloon.

The common loon is large. It weighs seven to nine pounds (3.1 to 4 kg) and measures 28 to 35 inches (71 to 89 cm). The common loon is about the size of the Canadian goose. Common loons living farther north are bigger than loons found in Minnesota and North Dakota.

The common loon's breeding feathers are black, checkered with white in a distinctive pattern down its back. It has a straight, heavy black bill and a black head. Its glossy, greenish-black neck is ringed with a white-striped necklace.

The common loon lives on lakes or deep rivers. It uses the plants that grow close to the water to hide its nest. The common loon is found from Alaska and Canada southward into the northern United States. In winter, the common loon migrates to the Atlantic and Pacific coasts and the inland Great Lakes.

The common loon keeps a watchful eye out for predators.

Purplish-black feathers decorate the neck of the arctic loon.

The arctic loon

Of all the loons, the arctic loon may be the prettiest. Its breeding feathers have the black-and-white checkerboard pattern of the common loon. Its black neck has long, curving white stripes, and its head is silver grey. Because of its purplish-black throat, it is sometimes called the black-throated diver.

The arctic loon's bill is smaller and straighter than the common loon's bill. The arctic loon is small. It measures only 23 to 29 inches (58 to 74 cm). It weighs four to five pounds (1.8 to 2.2 kg).

Arctic loons make noisy calls, especially during breeding. The call comes from deep in the throat and sounds like a wail or a yelp. If an arctic loon is frightened, it makes a high-pitched squeal.

During mating, arctic loons may chase each other around the lake, then splash and dive into the water. Sometimes in the summer, groups of adult loons will get together to play. They dive at each other, duck underwater, then lift into the air, slapping the water with their wings.

The arctic loon lives in the tundra (treeless plains), lakes, ponds, and marshes of Alaska and Canada. It winters along the Pacific Coast from Alaska to southern California and Mexico. Arctic loons are also found in Scotland, parts of Scandinavia, Russia, Japan, and Korea.

The red-throated loon

The red-throated loon is the smallest loon. It weighs only four pounds (1.8 kg) and measures 24 to 27 inches (61 to 69 cm). Some of its nicknames are the "little loon," the "pepper-shinned loon" (because of the speckled feathers by its legs), and the "rain-goose." It is one of the quieter loons, except during breeding.

The red-throated loon is easy to spot. While in its breeding feathers, this shy loon has a reddish-brown throat. Its grey-brown upper feathers are flecked with white. It is the only loon without the bold black-and-white checkerboard back pattern. The head and neck are grey with black-and-white stripes. Its bill turns up slightly.

The red-throated loon is the only loon that takes flight from the ground as well as from the water. Because of its smaller size, it needs less water on which to land and take off. Also, the red-throated loon does not dive as deeply as the common loon. For this

Because of its reddish-brown throat, the red-throated loon is easily identified.

reason, it can live on smaller lakes than its other loon cousins.

Red-throated loons fly farther north than other loons and are found in Canada, the United States, Europe, and Asia. Red-throated loons winter on Lake Michigan, along both U.S. coastlines as far south as Mexico and southern Florida, in the British Isles, and in parts of southern Europe and Japan.

The yellow-billed loon

The largest loon is the yellow-billed loon, sometimes called the white-billed loon. It measures 33 to 38 inches (84 to 97 cm) long and weighs 10 to 14 pounds (4.5 to 6.4 kg). That's three times heavier than the red-throated loon and two times heavier than the arctic loon. The curved bill of this loon is pale yellow. Otherwise, it looks very much like the common loon.

The yellow-billed loons' nests are big mounds of mud, much larger than the nests of other loons. Yellow-billed loons breed north of the Arctic Circle, where there are no trees and part of the ground is always frozen.

Yellow-billed loons live on large freshwater lakes and rivers in northwestern North America, from northern Alaska to Hudson Bay in southern Canada.

In winter, yellow-billed loons migrate to southern Alaska and British Columbia. Some fly down the California coast to the Baja (pronounced BA-ha) Peninsula of Mexico. In northern Eurasia, they are found from Finland to Siberia.

CHAPTER THREE:

Loons will eat almost anything that swims. Their diet is 80 percent fish, but the fish they eat have to be alive. Fishermen have watched loons turn away from dead minnows or fish.

Loons are big eaters. Like other birds, loons have to eat large amounts of fish to keep their body temperature the same (102 degrees Fahrenheit, or 30 degrees Centigrade) and to provide enough energy for diving, flying, and swimming. Scientists who have nursed injured loons back to health report that those loons ate 100 minnows a day! During the 15 weeks the loons are raising their two chicks, a pair of loons can eat one ton (907 kg) of fish . That's a small truckload of fish!

On freshwater lakes, loons usually eat perch, bullheads, sunfish, smelt, minnows, suckers, and sometimes trout and walleyes. But they will also eat frogs, salamanders, crayfish, and leeches. In salt water, loons eat sea trout, rock cod, flounder, and shellfish. If a lake holds few fish, loons, especially young chicks,

18

eat water plants, mollusks (soft animals with shells), and insects.

Some loons swallow big fish whole. Loons have a stretchy esophagus or throat pipe, so fish as big as two pounds (0.9 kg) can slide down their throats. But loons usually eat more frequent meals of smaller fish or minnows.

Loon parents take care of the young chicks for about 11 weeks after their birth.

How loons fish

A loon will peer down into the water and locate its prey by sight. Then the loon dives to grasp the fish in its long, sharp beak. That's why loons need clear water to feed. If the water is muddy, loons will feed on the bottom, going after slower-moving prey such as crayfish. Because they fish by sight, loons don't feed at night.

Loons usually swallow their prey underwater. But a fish with spiked fins or sharp scales can poke and prick on the way down the loon's throat. The loon takes a fish like that to the surface and breaks it into smaller pieces before swallowing it.

Strong swimmers and divers

Loons are expert swimmers and fast, deep divers. Fishermen have found loons entangled in fishing nets at depths of 200 feet (80 meters). Loons can stay underwater for up to five minutes. But they usually make shallow, shorter dives of less than a minute.

Surprisingly, the loon can float like a rubber duck on the surface, or it can drop into deep water like a stone. It can float on water because its waterproof feathers overlap, and air is trapped between them.

A loon spends many hours a day swimming, fishing, or just drifting in the water.

With its feathered air pockets, the loon floats on the surface like a balloon filled with air.

To sink below the surface, a loon must get rid of the air caught in its feathers. When the loon is ready to dive, it draws its feathers tight to its body, squeezing out the air trapped between its feathers. Loons also let air out of their bodies just before diving.

The body of the loon is meant for diving. Its legs are set far back and its body is long and narrow. A loon's big feet are flat, like blades, so they cut easily through the water. The loon's heavy bones help it sink into the water.

Loons swim easily. Their big feet push back and forth, toes closed. Underwater, loons are fast paddlers. When swimming or resting, loons ride low in the water. The water laps against their white breast feathers, about two inches (5 cm) below their neck markings.

Loons look for a quiet, secluded spot to build their nest.

CHAPTER FOUR:

Male birds are brighter and more colorful than the females. But male and female loons look exactly alike. Both loons wear the same beautifully-patterned breeding feathers.

Pairs of loons quietly glide across the surface of a lake or cruise together near shore, scouting for a nest site. Loon pairs often return to the nesting area they used the year before.

In fact, the nest may be what brings male and female loons together. Pairs of loons don't fly south for the winter together. But in the spring, they do move north in pairs. The male gets to the lake first. The female arrives a few days to a week behind him.

Loons have special ways of attracting each other's attention during mating. They show off by making short dives. They also show their throat patches to each other, preen their feathers, dip or flick their bills, rub their heads, or dive together in perfect rhythm.

Loons usually mate on shore, hidden from view. The male may signal to the female with a soft call. The actual mating takes only a few seconds. Once in awhile, a pair of loons will chase each other, skimming over the surface of the water. Then they'll dive together and mate underwater. They reappear on the surface after about 40 seconds. This underwater mating is less common than shore mating.

A messy nest

When they're ready to build a nest, loons look for a sheltered place near the water's edge. Deep water close to the nest is important, so the loons can dive for dinner and crawl back into the nest. The lake must have clear water and plenty of fish.

Loons will never win a prize for the most beautiful nests! A loon nest looks like a pile of weeds and dried leaves. Loons build messy nests out of any plant that grows close to the water. They'll use cedar boughs, marshy twigs, mud, and dry weeds. Both male and female help, but neither spends much time building the nest. From start to finish, the common loon spends just four to six hours building its nest.

Loons don't weave parts of their nest together. They just throw materials into a great pile and settle in. When it's finished, the nest can weigh as much as 40 pounds (18 kg).

Most common loons don't use their old nests, but start fresh with new materials. Yellow-billed and arctic loons may use their nests more than one year, so they build their nests more sturdily.

Loons build their nest out of twigs, leaves, mud, and weeds.

A frightened loon stays low and retreats into the water.

Sticking close to home

The female lays two long oval eggs about one inch (2.5 cm) apart in the nest. The eggs are olive brown with dark brown and black spots. The eggs are about twice as big as a chicken's egg.

For the next four weeks, the male and female loons take turns sitting on the eggs. This time of warming and waiting for the eggs to hatch is called incubation. During incubation, the blood vessels in the feathered pouches on both sides of the loons' breasts enlarge. This helps loons keep the eggs a warm 95 degrees Fahrenheit (35 degrees C), almost the temperature of the human body.

During incubation, one of the loons is always on the nest, and the other fishes close by. The nest-sitter carefully turns the eggs with its beak every so often and watches for unwanted visitors.

A nest-sitting shift lasts between a half hour and two hours. If its mate takes too long to fish, the other loon gives a loud call to remind it to come on duty! Once a loon parent enters the nest, it rearranges the eggs, then quietly settles in.

Protecting eggs is hard work. A loon usually sits in the "alert position," facing open water, with its head and neck sticking out. Occasionally loud motors or humans will frighten it off the nest.

Both loon parents take special care of their eggs.

Leaving the eggs alone gives egg-robbing animals the chance to sneak in and eat the eggs. Loons have to watch out for raccoons, crows, ravens, gulls, skunks, mink, otters, and sometimes muskrats and beavers. Under the best conditions, loons hatch two chicks each year.

The two loon eggs hatch a day apart toward the end of June. When first out of the eggs, loon chicks are covered with a thin tissue which they shed in the next few hours. Their feathers dry in 12 to 24 hours. Then the wobbly chicks follow their parents out of the nest and into the water. The tiny loons make low peeps like baby chickens. Chicks are much safer in the water than in the nest on the ground.

Loon chicks are born with soft downy feathers.

Grey downy chicks

All newborn chicks have mouse-grey, downy feathers with white markings on the upper breast and throat, and the undersides of their wings. For the first few days, chicks get piggyback rides, nestled in the warm feathers on their parents' backs. Chicks wait for the adults to sink low in the water, then climb aboard.

A day after hatching, chicks try shallow dives, about one foot (0.3 m) deep. But the chicks bob back to the surface like corks because of the air trapped under their feathers. After a few days, they can dive to a depth of ten feet (3 m).

Chicks can't catch their own food for at least a week after they hatch. The chicks are so hungry they need eight times as much food as adult loons. The parents feed the chicks as many as 75 times in one day! Fish, minnows, shell fish, and water plants are all part of a chick's diet. A chick begs for food by pecking at the parents' bills.

Chicks spend two to three months in their parents' care, seldom moving more than a few feet from the adults. During the early weeks, the chicks feed, preen, swim, rest, and ride on their parents' backs.

This closeness to their parents helps the chicks save energy and stay warm. It also protects the chicks from their enemies, like snapping turtles, hawks, eagles, and large fish. Gradually, chicks learn how to dive, fish, and "hide," by sinking low on the surface of the water.

After five or six weeks, the chicks are almost as big as the adults, and can dive to safety right along with their parents. At ten weeks, the chicks' downy grey feathers change to dull brown. When their flight feathers begin to grow, at about 11 weeks, the young loons are ready to leave their parents.

Young loons live on their own three to four years before mating and producing chicks. During that time, they must survive migration, harsh weather, disease, pollution, and other dangers.

CHAPTER FIVE:

Loons are powerful fliers. A common loon's wings measure almost five feet (1.5 m) from tip to tip. Their wings have to work hard to lift such heavy bodies into the air. Loons make long, flappy running starts on top of the water when they take off, then lift gradually into the air. Loons circle the lake a few times, climbing higher into the air each time around. Sometimes they call out as they fly.

Loons fly with their big feet straight back and close together. Their necks, breasts, and bills stretch forward like the nose of a plane.

Most loons prepare for their migration in late summer or early fall.

This narrowed shape lets the loon fly as fast as a speeding car, about 75 to 90 miles (120 to 145 km) per hour. Ducks and geese only fly 45 to 60 miles (72 to 97 km) per hour. Loons fly through strong winds and clouds, but won't fly in heavy rain or fog. Loons fly higher over land than water, sometimes as high as 7,000 feet (2,133 m).

Toward the end of summer, many loons get restless and move from smaller lakes to larger ones.

Loons must land on water. Some landings are smooth. The loon glides closer and closer to the water, then puts on the brakes with its feet and breast forward. But sometimes loons make funny crash

landings. They plop down on the water, their legs, neck, and wings going every which way. After landing, the loon often dives, then surfaces and flaps its wings before nestling down in the water.

Heading south

The migration of loons and other water birds is still a mystery. How do they find their way? Ornithologists, scientists who study birds, think loons steer by the sun or by the position of the earth. They may even use landmarks like rivers, coastlines, and mountains.

Loons migrate because of instinct. Instinct is a mysterious inner alarm clock which helps animals know what to do without having to think about it. Freezing temperatures force most loons to fly south to warmer areas in late summer and early fall. But a few hardy loons stay in the north until lakes freeze over in November. Some stay all winter on the cold open waters of the Great Lakes.

Loons start to get restless toward the end of summer. They move from smaller lakes to larger lakes. These serve as stopover places; there they meet other loons and flock together in groups of 100 or more. Loons fly south alone or in small groups.

Once in flight, loons head for the east or west coast of the United States, bound for the warm waters off Florida, California, or the Gulf of Mexico. They take advantage of tail winds blowing south to give them a push. They stop at favorite rest spots on the way.

The trip south is hard for some loons. They may hit bad weather on the way. Loons are helpless if they land by mistake on rain-slicked roads or parking lots instead of lakes or rivers. Loons are clumsy on land.

Loons rest at lakes and rivers along their migration route.

Unless someone rescues them and returns them to water, the loon soon dies. Other loons, especially young ones, sometimes wait too long to leave the northern lakes and get trapped on the ice, and die. Without their water runways, loons can't get up into the air.

A change in winter

In the winter, the loons' brilliant summer breeding feathers turn a drab dirt-brown or grey. Their haunting calls, which all summer sent ringing shivers across the northern lakes, are for the most part silent.

An individual loon spends about half its winter hours feeding, usually in the early morning and mid-afternoon. The warm ocean waters are full of fish, crabs, and other sea life, so less room is needed for each loon's feeding territory. Loons fish by themselves, but often spend the nights tucked into a protected bay. Loons nestle together in a huge "floating raft" in the evenings. When not feeding, the loons spend the daylight hours preening, drifting, and just resting.

Going north

In early spring, instinct tells the loons it's time to go home. Loons seem to sense when the northern lakes are melting. Instinct guides the loons throughout the hard journey back to their breeding grounds.

The loon leaves the warm waters of the south for the chilly north woods for good reasons. Loons run into more diseases, pollution, and violent storms on the seacoasts than up in Minnesota, Maine, or Canada. Fewer loons die in the summer breeding grounds of the north than in the winter coastal areas of the south. The peaceful northern lakes are less crowded, and the loons have more room to raise and feed their young.

Once they are close to their breeding grounds, a few loons fly ahead to "scout" for open water on the melting lakes. The scouts help the other loons arrive close to the time when the winter ice breaks apart. At that time there is plenty of landing room on the water.

Reaching the breeding grounds early is important. The summer season is short, and loons have much to do. They must stake out a territory, mate, make a nest, lay and incubate eggs. Then they must care for the chicks until they can fly and head south again before the lake freezes over.

In early spring, loons return to their breeding ground and prepare a new nest for their eggs.

CHAPTER SIX:

People cause many problems for loons. People like to use the areas where loons breed for boating, swimming, and fishing. People pollute the waters or frighten the loons away so they don't care for their eggs and their young. A loon may swallow a deadly fishhook or get tangled in garbage people throw into the water.

The loon is not an endangered species, but in many parts of North America, it is listed as "threatened," or on the "watch" list. That means that unless care is taken, the breeding grounds of the loon will continue to shrink, making the loon's future uncertain.

People help increase populations of raccoons and gulls by leaving behind garbage, fish tidbits, and other scraps. Despite a loon pair's careful guarding of the nest, raccoons and other animals kill many loon eggs. Gulls rob loon eggs, attack young chicks, bother nesting loons, and sometimes take over their nest sites.

Human hazards

During breeding and nesting, loons are easily disturbed. A roaring speedboat motor, noisy campers, a fishing boat, even a canoe, may frighten a loon off its nest. Loons become ill from eating fish infected with chemicals or harmful bacteria. Dangerous chemicals seep down into the ground, then flow into lakes, rivers, streams, and the ocean. These chemicals can cause shells of loon eggs to become too thin. Surviving loons may develop crooked bills, weak bones, or diseases.

Thousands of lakes have become polluted with acid rain, which is rain mixed with industrial air pollutants. This dirty rain poisons both the water and the fish loons eat.

The loons' nest must be close to the water to allow loons to slip easily in and out of the water. Dams in

During breeding and nesting, loons are easily disturbed.

Loons are adaptable and have learned how to live with humans.

places like New Hampshire or Maine sometimes make the water level go up or down. This changes the nest location, causing problems for the loon. A pair of loons might build their nest close to the water. But if a dam makes the water level rise, the water can wash away the loons' nest. If the water level falls, the loons may find their nest several feet away. Unable to pull themselves that far across the earth, the loons abandon their nest.

The good news

The good news is that loons are adaptable. Even though there are fewer breeding areas today, there are almost as many common loons now as there were 30 years ago. Some loons learn to live with people. They don't hurry away from their nests when startled, but sit on their eggs, no matter what.

In many places, naturalists are teaching people not to disturb nesting sites. Scientists place floating nests made of logs and water plants on lakes. These artificial nests give loons quieter areas to lay eggs and raise their young.

People love this beautiful northern bird. Loons don't need much to survive—just clear waters with plenty of fish, a protected nesting site near water, and a safe place to raise their young. The future of the loon depends on people's willingness to protect their habitats.

MAP:

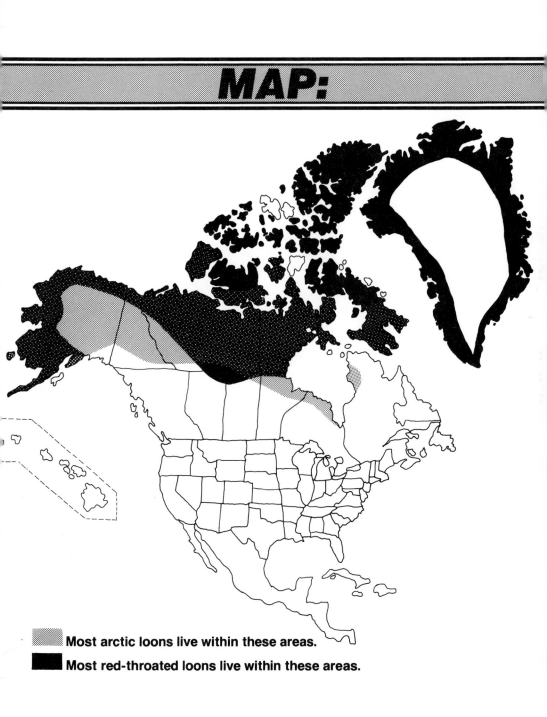

Most arctic loons live within these areas.

Most red-throated loons live within these areas.

MAP:

▨ Most common loons live within these areas.

▨ Most yellow-billed loons live within these areas.

46

INDEX/GLOSSARY:

47

WILDLIFE
HABITS & HABITAT

READ AND ENJOY THE SERIES:

If you would like to know more about all kinds of wildlife, you should take a look at the other books in this series.

You'll find books on bald eagles and other birds. Books on alligators and other reptiles. There are books about deer and other big-game animals. And there are books about sharks and other creatures that live in the ocean.

In all of the books you will learn that life in the wild is not easy. But you will also learn what people can do to help wildlife survive. So read on!